I Know I Can!
Bookshelf

ANTHEA DAVIDSON-JARRETT
Illustrated by
Aldana Penayo
Published by EDUCATE THE GLOBE,
London, UK, 2020.

ISBN: 978-1-913804-01-5

Copyright © 2020 Educate The Globe Limited. All rights reserved. No part of this book is to be reprinted, copied or stored in retrieval systems of any type, except by written permission from the author. Part of this book may, however, be used only in reference to support related documents or subjects.

I know I can do it!

Please can I help?

I want to do it all by myself!

Please can I try?

Can you show me how?

I'm not too small;

I am ready right now!

Daddy can you read to me?

I want to hear a story!

Please can you show me

the big man in the lorry?

Can we read another one?

You make reading fun.

You change the character voices

for every single one!

Oh dear! The cat got stuck

in the tall tree.

Move out of the way please!

The fireman's coming, see!

I'm happy the cat got saved

but can we read some more?

The fireman was very brave

and I like his uniform.

What's this one about?

Butterflies In The Meadow?

Ooh! The butterfly on her top

is my favourite colour; yellow!

Oh dear! Now all the

books are on the floor!

Let's organise

before we read some more.

How do we do it daddy?

"Start with A then B!"

"Ok, but. . . these two books start with C!"

"So then you look carefully

at the second letter.

Which of these comes first?

Take your time . . . no pressure!"

"Well the first book says 'Chips'.

The second one says 'Cones'

H comes before O...

I just did that on my own!"

"There are so many books.

Daddy. . . help me out!"

"Sure! You take A to M;

I'll sort the rest out."

"Ugh! What now?

Letters one and two are the same!

This one says 'Garden'

and this one says 'Games'?"

"Don't fret son!

Chill. Relax your mind!

When the letters are the same

keep going until you find.

letters that are different

then you work out

which comes irst in the alphabet.

It's not that technical!"

"Daddy you're so clever;

in fact you are the best!

Thank-you for showing me what to do

I want to do all the rest."

Ordering books is tricky;

stacking one by one but

I'm getting quicker every day.

This is so much fun!